JEREMY DYSON

Jeremy Dyson was born, raised and educated in Leeds. He studied Art at Jacob Kramer College, Philosophy at Leeds University and completed an MA in scriptwriting at the Northern School of Film and TV. In 1995 he formed the comedy group The League of Gentlemen with Mark Gatiss, Steve Pemberton and Reece Shearsmith. The League went on to enjoy a highly successful ten-year career, appearing on stage, radio, TV and film – winning, among others, the Perrier Award, the Rose d'Or, and Royal Television Society and BAFTA Awards for Best TV Comedy. In 2017 they came back together to make three special episodes of the show to celebrate their twentieth anniversary at the BBC. The specials were well received by delighted fans and were followed by a sell-out UK live tour in 2018.

In addition to his work with The League, Jeremy co-created the BAFTA-nominated comedy-drama series *Funland* (2005, with Simon Ashdown), was script editor and co-writer of BBC1's BAFTA Award-winning *Armstrong and Miller Show* (2007–2010), and co-creator, co-writer and director of Sky Arts' Rose d'Or-winning comedy series *Psychobitches* (2012–14). In addition he was script editor on the hit BBC shows *Grandma's House*, *The Wrong Mans*, *Bad Education* and the Emmy-nominated *Tracey Ullman's Show*.

Jeremy has written four works of fiction, *Never Trust a Rabbit* (2000), *What Happens Now* (2006), *The Cranes that Build the Cranes* (2009), which won the Edge Hill Award, and *The Haunted Book* (2012), published by Canongate.

In 2002 he made his first foray into directing – with a short film adaptation of Robert Aickman's *The Cicerones* for Film 4, an official selection at the Edinburgh Film Festival that year. In 2010 he co-wrote and co-directed with Andy Nyman the original production of *Ghost Stories*, which broke box-office records at the Liverpool Playhouse and Lyric Theatre, Hammersmith, before transferring to the Duke of York's and then the Arts Theatre in the West End, where it ran until 2015. In 2018, the film version of *Ghost Stories*, also written and directed by Andy and Jeremy, was released internationally to much critical acclaim, garnering a coveted 'Certified Fresh' label from the website 'Rotten Tomatoes', and a Fangoria Chainsaw Award for Best First Feature.

ANDY NYMAN

Andy Nyman has appeared in many films, including *Severance*, *Death at a Funeral*, *The Commuter*, *Judy* and *Jungle Cruise*. He won the coveted Best Actor Award at the 2006 Cherbourg Film Festival for his performance in indie movie favourite *Shut Up and Shoot Me*.

On television he has played an incredibly diverse range of roles, including Winston Churchill in *Peaky Blinders*, Jonty de Wolfe in Channel 4's cult comedy *Campus*, and Patrick in Charlie Brooker's BAFTA-nominated series *Dead Set*. Andy has also appeared in many plays, including Martin McDonagh's *Hangmen* and Mike Leigh's *Abigail's Party* in London's West End, and Stephen Sondheim's *Assassins,* and the lead role of Tevye in Trevor Nunn's acclaimed revival of *Fiddler on the Roof*, both at the Menier Chocolate Factory. *Fiddler on the Roof* transferred to the West End in 2019.

Andy has co-created and co-written many of Derren Brown's television and stage shows alongside Derren. Together they created some of the most notorious and popular TV of the past years, including *Russian Roulette*, *The System*, *The Heist* and *The Events*, including predicting the National Lottery result. Andy has also co-written and directed most of Derren's stage shows, including *Something Wicked This Way Comes*, which won them the 2006 Olivier Award for Best Entertainment, and *Secret*, which won them a 2017 New York Drama Desk Award.

In 2017 Andy and Jeremy Dyson wrote and directed the award-winning film of *Ghost Stories*, starring Andy, Martin Freeman, Paul Whitehouse and Alex Lawther. Among much acclaim it was voted the sixteenth Best Horror Film of All Time by *Empire Magazine*.

www.andynyman.com   @andynyman

Jeremy Dyson & Andy Nyman

GHOST STORIES

NICK HERN BOOKS

London

www.nickhernbooks.co.uk

A Nick Hern Book

Ghost Stories first published in Great Britain in 2019 as a paperback original by Nick Hern Books Limited, The Glasshouse, 49a Goldhawk Road, London W12 8QP

Ghost Stories copyright © 2019 Jeremy Dyson and Andy Nyman

Jeremy Dyson and Andy Nyman have asserted their right to be identified as the authors of this work

Cover design by Cog Design

Designed and typeset by Nick Hern Books, London
Printed in the UK by Mimeo Ltd, Huntingdon, Cambridgeshire PE29 6XX

A CIP catalogue record for this book is available from the British Library

ISBN 978 1 84842 826 3

Woodland
CARBON
www.woodlandcarbon.co.uk
NICK HERN BOOKS
Printed on Carbon Captured paper

Introduction
Jeremy Dyson and Andy Nyman

Ghost Stories is a dream come true.

We met in 1981 at a Jewish summer camp called, appropriately enough, 'Chai '81' ('Chai' being Hebrew for 'life'). It was fate that threw together three kids from Leeds (including Dyson) and three kids from Leicester (including Nyman) into one cramped room for six. We were fifteen and within a couple of hours had discovered that we shared two mutual loves: dirty jokes and a burning obsession with Horror. We became best friends, and in the thirty-eight intervening years very little has changed.

Over the years we've shared in every aspect of each other's lives: through adolescence, the trials and tribulations of dating, both moving to London, both getting married, both becoming fathers, both becoming middle-aged. Always sharing the ups and downs of life, always sharing laughs and news of the latest, greatest horror films.

Throughout our friendship we constantly mused, 'Wouldn't it be wonderful to actually work together?', always meaning it, but somehow never quite finding the time. We've both remained busy, Jeremy as a writer and Andy as an actor. Our careers, and the practicalities of being freelancers with families, meant the realities of collaborating were beginning to feel like an impossible dream.

Then one day that all changed. Andy was in the West End of London and happened to walk past the Fortune Theatre, where *The Woman in Black* has been playing for almost thirty years. Andy was struck by a thought: how insane it was that there hadn't been another horror play since that one had opened, almost as though such a thing wasn't allowed.

Andy had also recently seen *The Vagina Monologues* in which the staging is remarkably simple – three women sit on three stools reading/performing the play directly from the script. The two experiences collided and Andy phoned Jeremy with this thought – 'I think I know what we should work on together – a play, like *The Vagina Monologues*, but with ghost stories. Three men, sitting on three stools telling ghost stories.' Jeremy loved the idea and we started to ponder.

The third essential cog in the machine was Sean Holmes. He and Andy had worked together on a play Andy had starred in (*Moonlight and Magnolias* by Ron Hutchinson); they'd loved working together and wanted to collaborate on something else. Andy casually mentioned the idea of the ghost-story play. A month later Sean became the Artistic Director of the Lyric Hammersmith, and his second phone call on his first day in the job was to Andy, to find out what was happening with 'that ghost play'. A meeting was set for three days later.

Fortunately we'd been talking about it and thinking about it on and off for about a year, emailing each other fragments of our own writing and our favourite ghost stories by other people – so in some ways the earth had been tilled when we got together, prior to meeting Sean to drew up some rules of engagement:

- It had to be contemporary, so that it was as different as possible from *The Woman in Black*.

- It had to have a small cast to keep costs down.

- It should only be ninety minutes without an interval to keep the tension high.

- There should be no spoilers allowed at all, no plot given to press or indeed auditioning actors.

And finally, and most importantly:

- It had to be as frightening as the best modern horror film, with full 'leap out your seat' scares.

On 27 January 2009, we had the meeting and, incredibly, Sean and the Lyric commissioned the play, with us set to direct.

Sean's masterstroke, though, was programming the dates there and then that the play would open: exactly a year away.

We were both busy for about six months with our own various commitments, but set a time when we could get started properly. We sent each other thoughts, ideas and scribbles to keep the fires burning.

Then from the 19 July 2009, we finally sat down with four clear days to scratch out something concrete. The script had to be delivered on 1 October. The first thing we did was put a large index card on the wall. It said simply 'FUN', and it acted as an essential reminder both that the play itself should be entertaining and enjoyable, but also that the creative process wasn't to be some terrifying daunting task, but was built around the simple joy of two lifelong friends finally coming together to do what they had talked about doing for over thirty years.

We then set out with one very simple premise: what was the play we would most want to see ourselves? We started talking about our favourite moments from horror films, what made us laugh, scream and jump; but we also discussed what were the most memorable and impactful moments of theatre we could remember. The aspiration was somehow to combine both.

Very quickly the wall filled up with random thoughts and ideas, all disconnected but all born from the same place.

As we started to sift and shift these ideas into categories and sections, we realised that the 'three men telling three stories' idea had somehow shifted itself into a stage version of a cinematic phenomenon we both adored: the portmanteau horror film.

The incredible films of the production companies Amicus and Tigon in the 1970s, and their earlier 1940s Ealing Studios predecessor, *Dead of Night*, had shaped our childhoods – utterly British and yet fantastically global, full of deliciously playful scares that had creeped us out and stayed alive in our imaginations for decades. We knew, though, that we also wanted to craft a play that would deliver something of substance to an audience, some solid ground underneath the fun, that would leave a deeper, darker residue and be harder to shake off.

With that in mind, we asked each other a question: 'Had you ever done anything in your life that you were truly ashamed of?' The answers we gave would go on to shape both the individual stories and the overall plot in ways that were consistently surprising to us both.

* * *

Sean came to see us for a progress report and Andy performed a basic one-man version of the whole play for him. At that point, Sean suggested that as well as us directing, Andy should play Professor Goodman himself, truly a thought that had never occurred to us. Sean also told us that the play would now run for three weeks at the Liverpool Playhouse before moving to the Lyric. Very exciting news.

Incredibly, within three days, thirty years of friendship and a lifetime of absorbing horror had created the framework of the play. Many of the moments, scares and beats that we discussed then have remained unchanged over the subsequent years in which the play has been performed.

Another creative element that we were both very passionate about was that the show should also include something of our love of theme-park rides – that the story should somehow burst its banks and spill out into an immersive experience for the audience.

As you will see from reading the script, exactly what the experience of being in the theatre would be like was actually written into the show. We wanted to be playful with the form: What could the audience see around them? What could they smell? We also loved the idea that their involvement with the play would actually begin when they bought their ticket – with the purchaser being given a warning about how scary it was going to be by the box-office staff before they'd even handed over their money.

We delivered our first draft on 1 October 2009 and then kept developing and writing right though till day one of rehearsals – 11 January 2010.

* * *

Ghost Stories opened at the Liverpool Playhouse on 4 February 2010, and we truly had no idea what to expect. By now Sean had come on board as a third director, bringing a wealth of experience to help guide us through the technical rehearsals and first previews.

When the audience screamed for the very first time, it was one of the greatest moments of our creative lives. Something so unique and very special.

We continued to work on the play, learning from the audience, changing lines, moments and, in the case of the Tony Matthews story, the entire ending! It was a blissful time: doing the show in the evening, then staying up late, deconstructing what wasn't yet working, followed by our early morning 'porridge sessions', rewriting and problem-solving as we breakfasted.

The production moved to the Lyric Hammersmith where it started previewing on 24 February 2010. Wonderfully, it performed to packed houses and very swiftly transferred to the West End. It ran at the Duke of York's Theatre for thirteen months – a fact that still makes us pinch ourselves.

Since then the show has been performed all over the world – Moscow, Sydney, Lima, Germany, Toronto, Shanghai, Norway, Finland and with many more international productions planned. We also adapted it for film, writing and directing it ourselves. It was released in cinemas in 2018 both in the UK and internationally to much critical acclaim. It also won us a Fangoria Chainsaw Award for Best First Feature – a fact that would have made our fifteen-year-old selves explode with delight.

And here we are now, 2019. We are one week away from rehearsals for the revival of *Ghost Stories* at the Lyric Hammersmith, the final show of Sean Holmes's artistic directorship there. Like the best dreams, as one looks back and reflects on what has happened, it feels impossible, ungraspable. So many stars have to align to create anything, let alone something that lasts and is still a living, breathing thing almost a decade after it was first conceived. No small part of *Ghost Stories* success lies in the enthusiasm and individual brilliance of our fantastic creative team who threw themselves into the challenge of bringing it to life with a zeal that matched our own: Sean Holmes, designer Jon Bausor, lighting designer James Farncombe and sound designer Nick Manning.

It fills our hearts with joy that so many people have seen the show and kept its secrets.

We wish you the sweetest of dreams.

Ghost Stories was first performed at Liverpool Everyman and Playhouse on 4 February 2010, in a co-production with the Lyric Hammersmith. The cast was as follows:

MIKE PRIDDLE	Nicholas Burns
TONY MATTHEWS	David Cardy
SIMON RIFKIND	Ryan Gage
PROFESSOR GOODMAN	Andy Nyman

Directors	Jeremy Dyson and Andy Nyman
Associate Director	Sean Holmes
Designer	Jon Bausor
Lighting Designer	James Farncombe
Sound Designer	Nick Manning
Special Effects	Scott Penrose
Fight and Movement Director	Lewis Peploe

The production transferred with the same cast to the Lyric Hammersmith, London, on 1 March 2010, and to the Duke of York's Theatre, London, on 25 June 2010. From 8 November 2010 to 8 January 2011, the role of Professor Goodman was played by Reece Shearsmith.

It was revived at the Arts Theatre, London, on 13 February 2014, with the following changes to cast and production team:

PROFESSOR GOODMAN	Paul Kemp
SIMON RIFKIND	Chris Levens
MIKE PRIDDLE	Gary Shelford
TONY MATTHEWS	Philip Whitchurch

Fight and Movement Director Dino Fetscher

Ghost Stories was revived at the Lyric Hammersmith, London, from 29 March 2019. The cast was as follows:

TONY MATTHEWS	Garry Cooper
PROFESSOR GOODMAN	Simon Lipkin
SIMON RIFKIND	Preston Nyman
MIKE PRIDDLE	Richard Sutton

Directors	Jeremy Dyson, Andy Nyman and Sean Holmes
Associate Director	Joe Murphy
Designer	Jon Bausor
Lighting Designer	James Farncombe
Sound Designer	Nick Manning
Special Effects	Scott Penrose
Fight and Movement Director	Roly Botha

The Lyric Hammersmith first commissioned and co-produced *Ghost Stories* in 2010, taking the sell-out production on to the West End and Canada. The Lyric are delighted to be reviving the production almost ten years after its premiere.

For more than a hundred and twenty years, the Lyric has been responsible for creating some of the UK's most adventurous and acclaimed theatrical work. It has also gained a national reputation for its work with and for children and young people, and creates pathways into the arts for young talent from all backgrounds, helping to diversify our industry.

The Lyric's dual commitment to producing the highest-quality contemporary theatre, whilst nurturing the creativity of young people, is what makes it unique within the cultural ecology of the UK. It is a local theatre rooted in its community with a national and international reputation for the quality and innovation of its artistic work.

lyric.co.uk / @lyrichammer

Ghost Stories has also, at the time of publication, received international productions in the following countries:

Panasonic Theatre, Toronto, Canada, opened on 23 April 2011

Yauza Palace Theatre, Moscow, Russia, opened on 22 October 2012

Sydney Opera House, Australia, opened on 8 July 2015, followed by a tour to Geelong Performing Arts Centre, Victoria; the Space Theatre, Adelaide Festival Centre, South Australia; National Theatre, Melbourne, Victoria; Wagga Wagga Civic Centre, New South Wales; Canberra Theatre Centre, ACT; and the Heath Ledger Theatre, Perth, Western Australia

Teatro La Plaza, Lima, Peru, opened on 8 October 2015

Shanghai Modern Theatre, China, opened on 1 August 2018

Tampereen Komediateatteri, Tampere, Finland, opened on 3 October 2018

Characters

PROFESSOR PHILIP GOODMAN
TONY MATTHEWS, *late fifties/early sixties*
SIMON RIFKIND, *twenty*
MIKE PRIDDLE, *late thirties*

The audience pass into the auditorium through dark tunnels.

On the walls are random numbers, chalked at varying intervals: 6, 79, 19, 11, 92, 20, 48, 1, 32.

The tunnels are filled with a dreadful soundscape, subliminal at first, rising in intensity as they approach the theatre. The chalked numbers continue into the auditorium – under the balconies and all over the walls – a nightmarish feel and vision.

The drip-drip of puddled water and the whisper of distorted distant wind is everywhere. Not loud enough to be music, but present enough to unsettle.

Instead of house lights there are industrial temporary lights, cabled around the theatre, providing just enough illumination for the audience to find their seats.

The safety curtain is down, so none of the stage is visible. Polythene sheeting engulfs the pros arch. There is a lectern stage-right, sitting in a pool of light.

ANNOUNCEMENT (*gentle and polite*). Ladies and gentlemen, would you be kind enough to switch off your cellphones. We would ask that you refrain from texting or emailing during the performance. Photography or any sort of recording of the show is strictly prohibited. Please be aware that once *Ghost Stories* has commenced, should you leave the auditorium for any reason you will not be readmitted. Thank you for your cooperation.

The soundscape continues for another moment and then, with the suddenness of a blowing fuse – the lights snap out.

At the same second the lights blow a rasping wheezing begins – the frantic struggle for breath of a severe asthma attack. The sound fills the auditorium – surrounding the audience in the darkness. It is terrifyingly loud and intense.

The breath dies as suddenly as it started. A moment and then a grand orchestral theme begins. Timed to its rhythm a slide appears projected on to the gauze. Blurred at first we see it takes focus. A smiling family in front of a caravan. CLICK: A blurred sheet that appears to be dancing. CLICK: A number chalked on a concrete wall. CLICK: Philip Goodman's graduation photo. CLICK, CLICK: faster and faster – we are bombarded with these banal yet unsettling images. The music and images reach their conclusion.

Silence, then footsteps, a man walks through the auditorium and up onto the stage. This is PROFESSOR PHILIP GOODMAN *– he's confident, relaxed, pleased to be there. There's a breeziness and self-assurance to him.*

As he places his hands on the lectern, he knocks a pen off, which clatters to the floor.

GOODMAN (*under his breath*). Good start!

He bends down and picks it up.

Ghost stories. A very potent pairing of words. Ask yourself this. What is it that drew you to this event? If it's to discover what it is that scares you then the answer to that is easy – it's death and dying.

Beat. GOODMAN *has a darkness here, knowing he is challenging the audience.*

But that's not really why you're here. Is it? You're here to play a game with that fear. Why on earth would you want to do that? Why would you want to tease something that you know can make you feel sick to your stomach, that you know can keep you awake in bed at night worrying about what that creak from the next room is. Why would you want to play that game? Well the answer to that question is at the heart of the matter.

GOODMAN*'s tone now brightens. This is the start of the lecture proper and it is light, energetic and confident.*

My name is Philip Goodman and I'm a professor of parapsychology. My research looks at folklore and its relation to belief systems. So, if we disregard the world's most notable return from the dead in the world's biggest selling work of fiction –

GOODMAN *clicks a remote control at the screen and a picture of the Bible appears on the safety curtain behind* GOODMAN. GOODMAN *smirks to the audience, he knows this is cheeky.*

[*Throughout the lecture, it is* GOODMAN *who uses his remote to click on all the images and turn them off again.*]

– then the first historically recorded ghost stories appeared around 600AD when this man – Pope Gregory the Great – wrote his *Dialogues.*

A slide of Gregory the Great appears on the safety curtain behind GOODMAN.

…citing the appearance of spirits from beyond the grave, returning to warn those still living that unless they buck their ideas up – they'll roast in the fires of hell for all eternity.

So, naturally the Church embraces these convenient spirits, the stories are recycled, ad infinitum in weekly sermons with the sole purpose of maintaining good behaviour amongst the congregation.

GOODMAN *looks at the audience.*

You lot! These types of story remain pretty much unchanged up until the Reformation.

A slide comes up 'The Protestant Reformation (1517–1648)'.

(*Breezy.*) Stay with me! Post-Reformation, the Catholic Church loses its stranglehold on belief, the fire and brimstone falls out of favour and the ghosts become almost entirely secular. These new ghosts are much more about local narrative – a way of remembering and contextualising tragedy – a soldier fallen in battle, a wife murdered by her husband, a backwards child who died accidentally while playing an innocent game. These stories are transmitted orally – refined in the telling as they pass from village to village, generation to generation. The sixteenth, seventeenth centuries give us the rise of the printed word. The ghost story begins to appear in fiction, reaching its peak in the Victorian era...

A slide showing covers of the Victorian 'Penny Dreadful' booklets.

...Here it bleeds into the developing art of photography. Where the accidentally discovered phenomenon of the double-exposure gives us our first taste of spirit photographs –

A slide showing a 'double-exposure' spirit photography image.

And these images are only enhanced by the explosion of the motion picture and, inevitably, the ghost story appears on film.

The poster for the movie Dead of Night *comes up.*

What is fascinating is that no matter how society changes, or how sophisticated we think we become, these ghost stories adapt, they remain contemporary – their appeal – rather like their subject matter – refuses to die out.

Now, we don't want to give you all a fright, but I'm going to put the lights on.

GOODMAN *moves to the side of the stage by his lectern, and flicks a switch on the wall, turning the house lights on.*

By a show of hands – how many of you believe in ghosts. And by ghosts that does not mean Scooby-Doo, sheet-covered ghouls – it could be anything from the sensing of a presence right the way through to the spirit of a loved one coming back to offer you some comfort. Do you believe in ghosts? Hands up, don't be shy, tell the truth!

GOODMAN *takes in the audience response.*

Okay – that's roughly half of you. Half of you believe in ghosts. [*Or whatever the actual response is.*]

You can put your hands down. Thank you.

Okay, this time, only raise your hand if you believe that you have had an experience which could only be described as supernatural. Please keep your hands up.

A few hands go up.

The rest of you take a look around, you'll see that this is a much smaller number – a tiny minority in fact. And these few people who believe they've had a direct ghost experience – are known in the trade as 'percipients'. Thank you, you can put your hands down.

As the hands go down, GOODMAN *goes and flicks the switch, turning the house lights off.*

Three men sitting on a bench – a Frenchman, a Scotsman and a Jew. The Frenchman says 'I'm so tired and thirsty I must have wine.' The Scotsman says 'I'm so tired and thirsty I must have Scotch.' The Jew says 'I'm so tired and thirsty I must have diabetes.'

Beat.

Everybody has their version of the truth.

The word 'percipient' comes on the screen.

'Percipient.' You perceived the experience to be this – but it could have been that. As a scientist it makes proving anything actually happened virtually impossible. Everybody has their version of the truth.

A beat. GOODMAN*'s tone darkens a shade. He knows he is about to show the audience something they won't forget in a hurry.*

Let me show you something. In 2008 a fellow parapsychologist began the most comprehensive study of spirit photography ever undertaken. It's conducted online, it continues today, it's at scienceofghosts.com.

A slide 'www.scienceofghosts.com' comes up on the screen.

Anybody – and I genuinely do mean anybody – with a photo that they feel contains something anomalous or inexplicable is invited to submit it. As you can imagine, this brings a mixed bag of blatant hoaxes –

A first slide appears – an obvious hoax.

– obvious misreadings…

The second slide clearly a double exposure.

(*Sarcastic.*) …and some that are truly inexplicable.

The third is comically bizarre – a bearded man in a dress with talcum powder on his face and spiked-up hair.

But – from the many hundreds of photos submitted so far there is just one, that has given the researchers pause for thought.

The slide changes to be replaced by another – a seemingly ordinary photograph from a wedding.

This is a photograph from October 1972. It was taken at a wedding in Paisley, Scotland, by a professional photographer: from left to right William and Sandra Neilly and their friends Ann and Bob Hepburn. Now at first glance there appears to be nothing peculiar about the photo. But when the photographer made his enlargement he noticed something odd in it – and subsequently on the negative itself.

Subliminally a sound begins – a low and constant breath.

The Neillys had it examined by the official Glasgow police photographer. He stated unequivocally that the picture was genuine and not altered in any way. You should also know that the four guests, and the photographer all swear that they were the only people present at the taking of this photograph. Please bear that in mind, as we look at Bob's feet.

The slide is replaced with a blow-up of the part that features Bob's feet. GOODMAN *indicates the part he is talking about.*

There appears to be someone hiding behind him. Clearly visible here is a shoe – and the bottom of a trousered leg.

Perhaps even stranger is the face, peeping out from behind Bob's hip just here.

GOODMAN *uses a pointer to show the face hidden in the photo. It is a horrible, unforgettable image.*

Combine that face with the foot and we seem to have a man – possessed of a balding, middle-aged face, but with the gait and stature of a small child. Perhaps more troubling than that odd anatomy, is the expression of malign intent in that one visible eye.

As GOODMAN *say these last three words, the slide clicks in closer, closer and closer to the hidden face.*

GOODMAN *acknowledges the audience's reaction.*

Oh yes!

There's no doubt this is a striking and memorable image. But – but, but, but – does it constitute proof of 'the other side'? Let's take another look.

The wide-shot slide appears again.

Bob's hands are behind his back. Perhaps he's holding Ann's shawl in such a way that it has gathered to resemble a shoe and the bottom of a trousered leg. Perhaps? As for the face – take another look.

The close-up slide reappears on the screen.

Surely all I'm seeing is Bob's shirt cuff and watch strap creating the illusion of a face. But interestingly, despite these explanations, the brain still wants to believe.

GOODMAN *clicks the slide off.*

And you all demonstrated this when you put your hands up earlier – because although only a tiny minority of you believe you've had a direct ghost experience – a much greater number of you believes in ghosts. Why is that? Maybe it's because the brain, rather than accepting the mundane explanation of a mundane life, it positively chooses the colour and drama of a ghost story.

GOODMAN *adopts a mocking tone.*

A malevolent spirit perhaps seeking revenge on some
innocent person involved in an unfortunate accident or
whatever your particular story happens to be.

GOODMAN – *who has worked himself up into an excited
state – pauses, draws breath and returns to his lectern.*

In my twenty years of collecting ghost stories – or
'memorants', in the terminology of the folklorist – there
have only ever been three that have stood out to me as
unusual or different, certainly to the extent that they're the
ones I constantly replay as I lay in bed with nothing else to
occupy my mind.

The lights subtly go down, GOODMAN *is now at his lectern,
the rest of the stage in semi-darkness.*

The first of these stories came to me via an old schoolfriend,
Nico, Nico Freer. I bumped into him in the street, he'd heard
me on the radio being interviewed about what I was up to –
and he was reminding me of some of the dodgy stuff we –
like a lot of boys our age – got up to at school. Anyway it
was Nico who suggested that I interview –

GOODMAN *picks up his mini-tape-recorder and presses
play. White noise from the tape-recorder, then we hear the
dialogue. As we hear* TONY MATTHEWS' *first line, he
appears, lit through the safety curtain. The audience realise
that the curtain is actually a gauze, not the solid curtain they
imagined it to be.* TONY's *face is framed by the doorway of
a small cabin.*

The following exchange of dialogue comes off GOODMAN's
tape machine, which he plays into a microphone on his lectern.

TONY (*on tape*). Tony Matthews.

GOODMAN (*on tape*). Okay – so do you wanna tell me a little
bit about –

TONY (*on tape*). I don't think it's recording. The wheel's not
turning.

Noise of tape machine being picked up.

GOODMAN (*on tape*). No there is no wheel, it's digital. It is, it's recording. The red light's on. So do you wanna introduce yourself –

Over the course of the next lines of dialogue, lights come up on TONY *and down on* GOODMAN, *until we lose all light on the lecture.*

The gauze goes up as the lighting state shifts. This is the first time we are seeing the stage. It is mainly darkness but for a dimly lit night-watchman's cabin.

This is TONY MATTHEWS *– late fifties/early sixties, a lonely, bitter man. He is a weathered, working man. Whilst he is clearly beaten by life, there is still an occasional twinkle in his eye, the remnant of a charm that has been both his upkeep and his downfall.*

TONY *walks out of his cabin and downstage. He sits in a chair isolated in the middle of the stage.*

TONY. Who was it told you about me?

GOODMAN. Old friend of mine from school. Nico Freer.

TONY *scoffs.*

TONY. Old friend of yours? Is he hell. He's got less mates than me.

TONY*'s ability to cut through the bullshit jolts* GOODMAN.

GOODMAN. Regardless – Freer said you had an experience that might be of interest to me.

TONY. Oh yeah… 'Professor'. You know that's what they call someone who does a Punch and Judy show. A professor. Bet you didn't know that, did you?

GOODMAN. No – I didn't actually.

TONY. Well – look at that. The professor just learned something from a humble night-watchman.

GOODMAN. So that's what you do? You're a night-watchman.
   You always done that?

TONY. Course not. Left home when I was thirteen. University
   of Life, sunbeam. I've never stopped working and I ain't got
   a pot to piss in.

   GOODMAN *is now very dimly lit, deep upstage. We can
   barely make him out.*

   (*Rueful.*) Fairgrounds. Helter skelter – waltzers – always best
   for the ladies. Merchant seaman. Lorries – long distance.
   Market trader – fancy goods. Greengrocer. Lifeguard.
   Locksmith unofficial. Bouncer. Mechanic. Import, export
   unofficial. The list goes on.

GOODMAN. What about family? Are you married?

TONY (*snapping*). What difference does that make?

GOODMAN. Sorry – I'm not prying – it's just background on
   you – it's all part of how I classify my percipients.

TONY. Percipient? I didn't *perceive* this, sunbeam, I saw it with
   my own two eyes.

GOODMAN. Sorry.

   TONY *softens a little at* GOODMAN*'s apology.*

TONY. I was married to the same woman for fifteen years. You
   get less for murder, don't you.

   GOODMAN *laughs politely.*

GOODMAN. Did you divorce?

TONY. No she died, twenty-three years ago.

GOODMAN. I'm sorry.

TONY. We were kids when we got together. If she fell ill now
   they'd smash that cancer. Different world, isn't it.

GOODMAN. Any children?

TONY. You what?

GOODMAN. Any children?

TONY. How many more questions you got, Kojak? I've got a daughter Marnie, I've always loved Hitchcock. If it was a boy I'd have called him Norman! Marnie's not my wife's. Had a little bit on the side. What are you going to do?

GOODMAN. Do you see much of her?

TONY *looks at him.*

TONY. She's hospitalised.

GOODMAN. I'm sorry.

TONY. Sorry – why are you sorry – you didn't knock her down, did you? You apologise a lot. Got a guilty conscience?

GOODMAN *looks uncomfortable.*

She's been in there five years. 'Locked-in syndrome' they call it. Her eyes are open but everything else is paralysed. Coma – basically. The doctors don't know whether her brain's alive or dead. They say they can't begin to guess what's going on in her head. If I go and see her – no idea if she even knows I'm there or not. You very quickly get to the point where you think 'Why bother?' So I stopped going, couldn't handle it.

Beat.

Bloody hell I've depressed myself now.

A moment.

GOODMAN. Thank you for being so candid. So can you tell me about your – experience.

TONY. My experience. As the 'percipient', I can tell you this. I shat myself.

GOODMAN *laughs.*

GOODMAN. Please. Tell me everything. Everything that you can remember.

TONY. Everything that I can remember.

TONY *nods. As* TONY *starts to tell his story the lights fade on* GOODMAN. TONY *is now alone, just him, his cabin… and the darkness.*

I'd been a night-watchman in that depository for seven years. I used to call it the suppository because it was such a shit job. Lot of fellas didn't like it in there. Never bothered me. Place was near derelict, they'd been trying to get planning permission to turn it into a Tescos – cos there aren't enough of them! Place is pretty much empty – apart from stuff that's just been left there to rot – department-store surplus, piano parts. Gear that's not even worth nicking. Night-watchman's only there to keep out the squatters. They say that the place had been used as a 'what's-it' in the First World War – a nut-house in the First World War. Shell-shock and all that. One night-watchman, he swore blind he'd seen –

TONY *shakes his head, he doesn't complete the thought.*

You know what – it's all a load of tut. To me it was just a big old empty building.

It was my last night – it was a Wednesday night as a matter of fact, I was being replaced by some kid from Poland or Russia or Etonia or something. Now that is something to be frightened of, Polish kids coming over here working for peanuts!

TONY *stands. As he talks to us, he slowly moves from centre-stage into his cabin, taking his chair with him.*

It was quarter to four. Shit time of night. Even after seven years of doing the shift I hated that time. Your body never gets used to it. Like it knows it's wrong.

TONY *is now in his small night-watchman's cabin, it is poky and uncomfortable – he has a kettle, radio, computer and a three-bar heater which casts its orange glow over* TONY *and the room. Other than the cabin's little pool of light – the stage is pitch black.*

TONY *fills in a little printed log that's on a clipboard hanging on the wall. Sits down. SCREECH – a horrible metallic shrieking sound splits the silence.* TONY *picks up his walkie-talkie.*

Hello?

The walkie-talkie screeches again.

Hello? Marek? You've got to press the button on the side.

He waits for response. Nothing.

(*Into the walkie-talkie.*) Press the big black button on the side.

…Russian prick.

MAREK (*through walkie-talkie*). Hello, Tony. I'm in other building.

TONY. Congratulations. Which other building?

MAREK (*through walkie-talkie*). The other one.

TONY. What colour is the door?

MAREK (*through walkie-talkie*). Blech – Er blue.

TONY. Alright – you're in building number three.

MAREK (*through walkie-talkie*). Three, yes, what do I do?

TONY. You sit on your arse for the next ten hours and every two hours you go for a walk round and then chart it. Set the timer I gave you. Other than that do what you want, read, play chess, learn English.

MAREK (*through walkie-talkie*). Okay, thank you a lot, Tony.

TONY *puts the walkie-talkie down. Picks up a thermos flask of tea and fills a mug from it.*

As TONY *puts the lid back onto the flask, the lights dip momentarily. He opens a carton of milk, sniffs it – the milk is off. He throws the carton into the bin in disgust.*

He sits for a moment. TONY *then types a web address on the keyboard and waits.*

TONY. Evening, ladies…

TONY's eyes wander across the screen. We can't see what he's looking at. He makes his selection.

He stares at the screen, light from it illuminating his face. Sound begins. He's watching porn. Miniature groans and grunts fill the air. We stay with this for longer than is comfortable.

TONY *continues to watch passively, sipping his tea and dunking a biscuit until the scene reaches its inevitable conclusion. The sounds are disturbing.*

TONY *checks his watch. He puts the radio on. A talk-radio station.* TONY *picks up a Sudoku whilst it plays.*

We hear a late-night talk-show host speaking. [We don't hear this first part of the dialogue, this is for reference only: 'You're right – I think that's certainly romantic – chocolate – but what about flowers? I remember years ago giving an old g–…']

RADIO DJ.…–irlfriend of mine lilies. And she said thanks a lot – you know they give me a headache. It had the opposite effect to what was intended. Have you ever tried to do something romantic that's got you into deep water with a loved one? Or maybe you just want to tell us what you think love is. Give us a ring. Mike in Barnet – hello?

CALLER 1 (MIKE). Hiya, Jeff – yeah – it sounds silly – but you know, for us, it's getting a Chinky on a Saturday night, slobbing out in front of the telly. Just feels like love to us. We don't need anything else.

RADIO DJ. Thank you for that, Mike. You mean a Chinese of course, don't you. Apologies on Mike's behalf. But you're so right. There's nothing better is there. Slobbing out on a Saturday night with a takeaway pizza – and some rubbish on the telly. Ah heaven. Heaven.

Oh, on line three – I see we've got, oh, it's one of my girlfriends – hello, Betty. Hello, darling, how are you?

CALLER 2 (ELDERLY WOMAN). I'm lovely, Jeff. You know
– people seem so concerned these days about 'you've got to
have this and you've got to have that' that they forget the
simple things. You know like holding hands. My husband
had a stroke a few years ago and he's been bedridden ever
since. But I see him every day without fail. I hold his hand
and tell him what's going on. Even if it's just silly things –
what I had for breakfast. Even though he can't respond I
know that somehow he's taking it in – because love has a
way of conquering – [*We don't hear these last few words, the
radio is cut off before.*]

TONY *springs to his feet – aggressively turns the radio off.*

TONY. Like that makes you a saint. Silly old bitch.

TONY *finishes his tea. Checks his watch.*

Thank Christ for that.

Time for a walk-round. TONY *grabs a torch and steps out of
his cabin. Two steps into the darkness and…*

*SCREECH. The walkie-talkie wails. He's left it in his cabin.
He goes back to pick it up.*

Hello.

Nothing. TONY *is exasperated.*

Press the black button, Marek.

MAREK (*through walkie-talkie*). What time is it?

TONY. Christ. It's a quarter to four. You need to buy a watch.

MAREK (*through walkie-talkie*). I'm wearing one, it is broken.

TONY (*to himself*). 'Kin' hell.

MAREK (*through walkie-talkie*). I not like this place, Tony.
It feels bad. We have word for this back home. It is *złośliwy.*

TONY. Get yourself a radio, sunbeam, yeah. Get yourself a
radio. I'm going on a walk. Sit tight for ten minutes. I'll call
you when I'm back.

MAREK (*through walkie-talkie*). Okay. Thank you a lot, Tony.

TONY (*warmer*). That's okay, son.

TONY *goes to his little CD player – selects a CD from the handful that are there. Pops it in and presses play.*

The haunting tinkle of 'Why' by Anthony Newley begins.

As TONY *starts venturing down the dark corridors, the sound of the music and safe glow of the lights from his cabin fade.*

TONY *walks down the corridor. He reaches three huge, heavily padlocked doors, each with a light above them, barely illuminating the doorway. He goes to the first door, it has a big number '6' chalked onto it. He checks the padlock, shakes the door in frame. It is secure. He walks on.*

He reaches the second door, number '79' chalked onto it. He repeats the procedure. This door too is secure. Anthony Newley is still dimly audible, echoing in the distance.

Onto the third door, number '19'. Once again it is secure. Job done. TONY *starts the walk back towards the safety of his cabin, Anthony Newley getting louder as he approaches.*

TONY *pauses on his way. Pops his torch onto the floor so its beam is directly up at* TONY, *underlighting his face. He rifles through his pockets and removes a packet of fags. He pops a fag in his mouth, takes a lighter from his pocket and lights it – as he does so the distant music suddenly distorts.*

TONY *is lost in his thoughts. He goes to light his cigarette. The small lights above the locked doors all flicker off.* TONY *moves his lighter to the cigarette and just as he reaches it, from the back of the audience we hear –*

LITTLE GIRL'S VOICE. Daddy.

TONY *spins around startled. He picks the torch up, shines it frantically around the auditorium looking for the little girl who called out. There's nothing there.*

TONY. Hello? Hello hello?

TONY *swings his torch around upstage. As he does the beam of his torch catches a* FIGURE *deep upstage behind him – a dummy like a little girl, but bigger. Red dress, porcelain pale-white arms, jet-black pigtailed hair and a china-doll face – distorted and very, very disturbing.* TONY *doesn't see her.*

This is 'TILLY'.

TONY *stands, still flustered from hearing 'Daddy'. He shines his torch, looking, this time, into the area where the figure's just been seen. There is nothing there now.*

TONY *pulls himself together. Gets back to his cabin as quick as he can, not running, but moving briskly, hiding his fear from himself.*

He gets back, turns the CD off. He chooses another CD, puts it on and hits play. Nothing. It doesn't play. He tries the computer. This is dead too. He tries the radio. A burst of white noise with a disturbing wheeze under it. Then the sound of male voices.

MALE VOICE 1. It's a coma, a probable 'lock-in'. Here for keeps…

MALE VOICE 2. Just one of those things.

TONY *flicks it off then tries turning it on again. This time it goes dead.*

BANG BANG BANG on the cabin door. TONY *freezes.*

TONY. Hello…

No response.

Marek?

TONY *cautiously opens the door, steps out. There is no one there. He turns to go back in.*

BANG. SLAM. The sound of a huge, heavy door crashing shut in the distant corridor.

Fuck!

TONY *tries the walkie-talkie.*

Marek? Marek?

There is no answer from MAREK. *Just a horrible white noise with yet another horrible wheeze pushing through the static, then over the walkie-talkie: 'DADDY'.*

He picks up his torch and cautiously steps out again.

He sets off – if kids have broken in, they'll pay. TONY *comes to the first door. Locked. The second door. Locked.*

The third door. TONY*'s torchlight moves from the door's number to the padlock, the second the light catches it the padlock and heavy chain drops to ground with an almighty clatter.*

Beat.

The door slowly creaks open. TONY *takes a shaky step towards it. From behind the door we hear.*

LITTLE GIRL'S VOICE. Daddy!

TONY. Hello? Who's there?

TONY *takes a deep breath. He pushes the door open, he's ready for it.*

He swings the torchlight ahead of him as he enters the room.

The torch beam hits a face. TONY *jumps. It is a little-girl dummy in a red dress, she looks like the glimpsed* TILLY *doll from earlier.*

He turns a dim light on. In the dirty light of the forty-watt – we can see the place is full of mannequins – a fifties broken-down feel to the dummies. They've been there for years. Some broken. Some wearing make-up. Some half-dressed. Some whose faces seem to be screaming. All of the mannequins are bald – without hair or eyebrows. At the back of the mannequins is the TILLY *mannequin.*

There are a few shop-display units. In amongst the dummies is what looks like another dummy with a sheet draped over it.

As TONY*'s torch hits this covered figure, there is the slightest movement from beneath the sheet.* TONY *sees this and knows he has the intruder.*

You stupid bastard!

TONY *reaches out and whips the sheet off.*

Beneath it is just a mannequin. This one is strange, however. It's a male dummy wearing a distinct bright-green hospital gown and an elasticated hospital hairnet. There is a name-tag round its wrist.

TONY *doesn't like it. He's seen enough. He picks up his torch. Suddenly the door slams shut. He runs to the door to get out, but it is locked.* TONY *is panicking.*

Hello? Hello?!

The lights flicker and go off.

TONY *moves forward, shining his torch around, shaken. In the darkness we hear:*

LITTLE GIRL'S VOICE. Daddy.

TONY *flicks the torch on, hitting the* TILLY *mannequin which is now standing centre-stage.*

TONY *frantically swings his torch back to the door, he must escape.*

Daddy.

TONY *swings his torch back to* TILLY. *The second the torch beam hits her,* TILLY *suddenly moves towards* TONY *as the sound builds to a crescendo.*

Daddy, Daddy, Daddy, Daddy!

The final image we see is TONY *frozen in the locked room as the hideous* TILLY *doll reaches its arms out for her daddy.*

BLACKOUT.

Slowly a light comes up on GOODMAN *at his lectern. The safety curtain is back in.*

TONY (*on tape*). Without a word of a lie, that's how it happened, sunbeam.

GOODMAN *clicks off his mini-tape-recorder.*

GOODMAN. Now – none of us were there on that night, so we only have Tony's word for what actually happened. He 'perceived' that dummy move and say to him 'Daddy'. And who knows – that may well be exactly what happened.

(*Mocking*.) Maybe the spirits crossed over from the other side – rearranged the very atoms and molecules of that dummy and loaned it the gift of speech. Or consider this – here is a decent hard-working man. He's suffered more than his fair share of tragedy and is trying to live with the fact that, up until that night, in the five years since his daughter's been comatose – he has only visited her twice.

So which is more likely? The dummy receiving a moment of spiritual animation, or the slow drip-drip of guilt mixing with Tony's fear, loneliness, exhaustion and rage? Real or not – what matters is Tony's interpretation of the event. Tony told me, the day after the incident he started visiting his daughter again.

According to Tony, the doctor said that despite her comatose state, when Marnie heard her father's voice for the first time in almost five years – her heart skipped a beat.

Beat.

GOODMAN *brings up a new slide – '51%'.*

Fifty-one per cent. That's the proportion of the world's population that is currently online. According to the 'Internet World Statistics Study' that provided that figure, twenty-two years ago it was only nought-point-four per cent. That means that now more human beings are online than offline. Now that is a remarkable thought. Gone are the days where a story that captures the imagination goes from village to village, growing and ch–

Abruptly GOODMAN *just stops. It's as though someone pushed his pause button. His lifeless arm drops to his side,*

his face drops, his eyes roll and his head flops back. He takes
two grisly breaths. As suddenly as he's stopped – he starts
again – perfectly normal as though nothing has happened,
the whole sequence lasts no more than a couple of seconds.

…changing as it does. Now that same story can potentially
touch half of the planet in the speed of a mouse click.
These new ghost stories often come to us quite
unexpectedly, an email pops through from a friend, it has
the most innocuous of subjects, 'Is this real?', 'What is
this?', 'Have you seen this?' You innocently click on the
link to a page that has a brief story followed by a video.
The story generally goes something like this. In some
far-off foreign land a teenage girl is listening to loud
modern music on the radio and her mother demands she
turns the music down. When the girl ignores her, as
teenagers are wont to do, the mother reaches for the 'Holy
Book' to show her that the Lord makes it clear young girls
must respect their parents in all things. Having heard this
a thousand times before, the girl storms off to her bedroom,
as teenagers are wont to do, but this time as she leaves she
grabs the 'Holy Book' from her mother's hands, throws it
to the floor. The distraught mother is furious and leaves the
insolent girl to stew in her bedroom all night long. But
when the mother goes to check on her the next morning,
well… what she found has become the stuff of legend.

The clip I'm about to show you has been viewed over two
million times on the internet and, like the Neillys' ghost
photo, it's absolutely real. This is footage of that girl today,
a girl punished for her blasphemy by a vengeful god, who
must now spend her miserable life on display as a warning to
others. Some of you will find this disturbing.

GOODMAN *clicks on his remote control and video footage*
is projected on the screen behind him.

Snake-woman video: The real internet video is now played.
It is shot on a mobile phone and is poor quality – it starts
with someone approaching a farm hut, the sun is bright and
says 'foreign land'.

The walk to the hut is over. Inside, behind chicken wire, displayed on a grimy mattress, lies the creature. The mobile camera moves closer to the wire to get a better look. It is wretched-looking, in filthy rags.

What is it? Is the bottom half an animal? A raccoon or a dog? The face seems human – miserable, bloodless, horribly aware of its own plight. What it once was, knows it is being watched and stared at. Its flipper-like limbs twitch and jerk. It moans in distress.

All that is audible is the indecipherable jabber of the people watching, and the occasional pained sound from the creature itself.

FREEZE ON THIS IMAGE.

Except, what we actually are seeing, ladies and gentlemen, is pure circus! A ruse, a trick, created in 1842 by the greatest showman that ever lived, P. T. Barnum. I present for you, the Fiji Mermaid, half-woman, half-beast.

As GOODMAN *talks, images of P. T. Barnum and the bunkum of which* GOODMAN *speaks flash up on the screen.*

Barnum's version was the head of a monkey grafted onto the body of a large fish, later sideshows added the expertise of the magician and presented living, breathing versions of the same illusion.

Images of these wondrous 'seaside attractions', 'The Headless Woman' in action, plus copies of plans how to make these illusions.

'The Headless Women', 'Spidora, half-lady half-spider' and now what do we have? 'The insolent dog-girl who disobeyed her parents and her god.' Roll up, roll up! Step inside, alive, alive, alive.' Barnum would be proud.

GOODMAN *becomes heated, disproportionately passionate.*

How… how can it be that rational, thinking adults could respond to such patent childish nonsense as if it were fact.

Newsflash! Hell does not exist! Heaven does not exist.
Where are these magical lands?

We might as well believe we take the second star on the right
then go straight on till morning! Why should we worry about
these ridiculous invisible storytime realms. This –

GOODMAN *bangs the lectern.*

This is real, this is now. This is where matters.

*He takes a sip of water – he whispers something, sharing
a joke with himself.*

I received a letter from a young man by the name of...

GOODMAN *picks up his mini-tape-recorder again.*
GOODMAN *presses play. The audio begins.*

SIMON (*on tape*). Simon Rifkind...

GOODMAN *turns off the tape.*

GOODMAN. Simon was seemingly confident, extremely
well-educated and from a stable middle-class background.

What made him extraordinary?

The extremity of his story...

GOODMAN *starts the tape-recorder again. As the sound of
the interview starts, the lights fade on* GOODMAN *and
come up on* SIMON RIFKIND.

*He is standing behind the safety curtain. He is twenty,
fresh-faced but with a terrible nervous edge. He looks
sleep-deprived and haunted.*

Thank you for writing to me.

SIMON. I'm so grateful you're here, sir, and I really appreciate
the fact that you've come to me. My parents said I should
have come to you, but I don't like going out... So many trees.

SIMON *laughs apologetically.*

That must sound mad to you.

(*Reacting to tape-recorder.*) You're not recording this, are you, sir.

GOODMAN. I was going to, yes.

SIMON. Who gets to hear it?

GOODMAN *appears dimly lit deep upstage.*

GOODMAN. Well that's entirely up to you. If you give me permission, students – people who attend lectures. If you'd rather it remained confidential, it'll remain confidential. Just let me know what you're happiest with. For now – it's just about me having an accurate record of your ghost story.

SIMON. This isn't a ghost story, sir.

GOODMAN. Okay. So what is it?

SIMON. If I knew that I might not be – I wouldn't have had to write to you… Sorry, I'm sorry. It's just – that's what I need you to tell me.

(*Suddenly perturbed.*) Are you going to be able to help me with this, sir?

GOODMAN. I won't be able to offer you any concrete solutions, if that's what you mean. But what I can tell you is that everything I've ever encountered has had a rational explanation.

SIMON. I don't want diplomacy, sir. I want you to help me understand what I saw that night.

GOODMAN. I'm sorry. I don't know that I'll be able to do that.

SIMON (*distraught*). What good are you then!

GOODMAN. Simon – you wrote to *me* inviting *me* here.

SIMON *cuts across him, he's becoming enraged.*

SIMON. Exactly – I wrote to you because when I heard you on the radio, you sounded like you knew about this stuff. You called it 'your area of expertise'.

GOODMAN. Listen – I feel we may have got off on the wrong foot. I might be able to throw some light on to it for you, I don't know yet, that's all. What do other people think of your story?

SIMON. I've never told anyone else.

GOODMAN. Okay. How sure are you that you're still remembering the incident as it happened?

SIMON. How sure am I?

GOODMAN. People tend to misremember as time goes by. They embellish.

SIMON*'s voice is suddenly filled with dread and terror.*

SIMON (*crazed and whispered*). I'm not embellishing anything. Think of a moment in your life that fills you with absolute dread.

GOODMAN*'s face flashes – a flicker of 'something'.*
SIMON *notices the look on* GOODMAN*'s face.*

There you go. Yeah! I'll bet when you close your eyes and think about that terrible moment, you can remember every detail of it, as if it's happening right now. That's how I know I'm not embellishing –

GOODMAN (*cutting* SIMON *off*). Please! Just tell me about the incident.

SIMON *takes a breath – telling this story isn't easy for him.*

SIMON. I don't know where to start.

GOODMAN. How about the beginning. Where are you?

SIMON. I'm in the car.

GOODMAN. And are you parked? Are you driving?

SIMON. I'm driving home.

GOODMAN. Right. And where had you been.

SIMON. A party – at Eddie Leviten's house. At a friend's house. It was about an hour from home. Dad had lent me his car.

GOODMAN. Anyone in the car with you?

SIMON (*answers too quickly*). No, I never gave people lifts.

GOODMAN. Really? Why not?

Pause.

SIMON. Look –

This is clearly difficult for him.

For about a year I was driving without a licence.

GOODMAN. Without a licence?

SIMON. I don't know why or what happened but when I got home – after failing my test – and my mother asked me 'Have you passed?' I heard myself say 'yes'.

SIMON *almost laughs, incredulous at his own story.*

I don't know why. Maybe I didn't want to let them down. I don't know. But once it was out there, I couldn't take it back. I guess I thought I'd just retake it in secret. I never did. I absolutely hated going out in the car, I avoided it, especially at night. But this was the last party where everyone was going to be together before going off to uni. And it was the only way I could get there.

BLACKOUT.

The ring of a mobile. It keeps ringing as we hear a door slam and the engine of a car kick into life.

Suddenly we are blinded by the headlights of a car driving towards us. After a second the headlights fade a little, and we now see SIMON, *sitting at the steering wheel of his dad's car, driving with noticeable caution. The phone keeps ringing.*

He looks down, terrified of taking his eyes off the road. He frantically holds the phone up to his ear. Even though he is talking normally on the phone we hear the other side of the call loud and clear.

As he drives we hear the sounds of the car whilst the lighting and design suggest his passage along a lonely country road.

MUM (*on phone*). Where are you?

SIMON. I'm in the car. I'm driving home.

MUM (*on phone*). Thank God.

(*Off.*) He's in the car, Raymond.

(*To* SIMON.) We've been trying to call you. Where have you been?

SIMON. Sorry, there's no reception near Eddie's.

MUM (*on phone*). We've been sitting here on shpilkes. You should been have back hours ago.

DAD (*on phone, in background*). You should have been back hours ago.

MUM (*on phone*). Raymond, for God's sake – I'm talking to –

The phone cuts off. SIMON*'s lost reception. He keeps driving. He picks the phone up and looks at it. Still no reception.*

After a moment's more overcautious driving, a message pips through on his phone. SIMON *looks down, desperate not to look away from the road. He grabs the phone. Sighs in exasperation and clicks listen.*

PHONE. You have one message. Message received 3.44 a.m.

DAD (*on phone*). Your mother said you just put the phone down on her. I suggest if you ever want to borrow the car again you give us a ring –

PHONE. To save the message press one. To delete the message press two.

SIMON. Two.

Resigned, SIMON *dials. The phone barely rings before picked up.*

DAD (*on phone*). Hello.

SIMON. It's me.

DAD (*on phone*). Your mother's gone to bed. We are very upset.

SIMON. Dad, I didn't put the phone down on her, I'm sorry I'm late.

DAD (*on phone*). I just found your bloody housing form for university – that you should have sent in three weeks ago. You told me you'd sent it.

SIMON (*pained*). I thought I had sent it.

DAD (*on phone*). You're a bloody liar –

The phone cuts off.

SIMON (*to himself, exasperated*). Shit!

The phone rings again. Still keeping half an eye on the road, SIMON *answers it.*

DAD (*on phone*). When your brother was going off to university he had two jobs in the summer before he left. He was doing the meat round for Katz's in the days and at night he was schlepping carpets for Ronnie Sacks in the warehouse. He applies himself, and you leave forms three weeks longer than they should be. You're a waster. Don't tell me you haven't got time.

SIMON*'s heard this a hundred times.*

SIMON. Please. Dad. It's quarter to four in the morning.

BOOOMPHHH! BANGGGG! A SCREECH OF BRAKES!

Something has dashed in front of the headlights, been hit hard by the car and flung over the bonnet.

In the briefest of glimpses that the headlights allow, we see a flash of what the car has hit – a little man's body, pale skin and long straggly white hair. And was that a goat's face?

What was it? Whatever it was, it was wrong. And now it's lying, fucked, at the back of the car.

SIMON *sits there, engine running, taking it in.*

Oh my God! Oh my God! Oh my God!

He's on a deserted country road, surrounded on all sides by skeletal trees, which stretch back into a dense dark forest.

He waits a moment longer before taking off his safety belt.

He opens the car door and steps out, the ping-ping-ping of the open-door alert echoing in the silence.

He steps out tentative, terrified.

(*Pathetically.*) Are you okay?

Gradually he edges his way around to the back of the car.

In the blood-red of the rear lights we see his horrified face. He looks down, sees what he's hit.

And then SIMON *pukes.*

SIMON *quickly gets back into the car.*

He frantically searches for a bottle of water. Finding one, he takes a sip.

He picks up his phone and dials. We hear it ring for a second and then it's answered.

PHONE. Hello Emergency Services, which service do you require.

SIMON *rethinks and quickly cuts the call off.*

It's another moment of madness, like lying about being able to drive. He is a boy in a man's world. What's he going to do?

He makes his decision. He gets into the car, throws the phone down, slams his door closed, puts his foot down and drives.

As the car pulls away at speed, SIMON *seems both panicked and relieved. Happy to be putting distance between him and the accident.*

Then we see something SIMON *doesn't – tiny, just visible in the fading red of* SIMON*'s tail lights – we see a flash of white hair, pale skin and a tiny figure springs to its feet.*

SIMON *drives and drives and drives.*

And the fog rolls in, engulfing SIMON*, the car and the audience.*

The engine chokes and dies.

SIMON. No no no no no no no.

He tries the ignition a couple of times. The sickening rise and fall of the engine attempting to fire. Is that an asthmatic whisper we can hear beneath the damp carburettor?

SIMON *turns on the internal light. It's weak and flickery. He picks up his phone to dial. No reception! He opens his window and sticks his arm out searching for signal… Nothing. Shit – he has to do something. Terrified, he clicks his car door open, waits, and then moves quickly looking for reception. Still nothing!!!*

Fucking O2.

SIMON *suddenly finds a signal and dials. The phone is answered.*

MUM (*on phone*). Well?

SIMON. Mum – it's me.

MUM (*on phone*). Are you okay, doll!

SIMON. I'm fine. I'm fine.

MUM (*on phone, frantic*). You're not, I can tell in your voice.

SIMON. I'm fine. Listen to me. The car's broken down.

MUM (*on phone*). Oyah clog! I'll bet it's foggy.

SIMON. Yeah, it is foggy.

MUM (*on phone*). That bloody car.

SIMON. Mummy. What should I do?

MUM (*on phone*). Don't worry, doll. Call the breakdown. The number's on the windscreen. Will you ring and let me know you're okay?

SIMON. Of course I will. Mum, I love you.

MUM (*on phone*). I love you too.

He hangs up the phone, looks on the windscreen, finds the number for National Breakdown and dials.

CALL CENTRE (*on phone, cheery phone voice*). Hello. National Breakdown. Can you give me the car's registration please?

SIMON. It's EE53 0HD.

CALL CENTRE (*on phone*). Thank you. And is that Mr… Rif… Rif… Rif –

SIMON. Rifkind. I'm his son. Simon.

CALL CENTRE (*on phone*). Okay, Simon. And are you with the car right now?

SIMON becomes distracted. He lowers the phone as he looks around.

Hello, Simon.

SIMON. Sorry – Hang on a second –

Beat. A sudden twig snap. SIMON swings round, what the fuck!!! He cowers.

(*Whispers.*) Yes. I'm right by it.

CALL CENTRE (*on phone*). Okay – you'll be happy to know that your father's a premium member – so you're covered – and we have you on the GPS. So we know exactly where you are and we'll be with you in somewhere between ten and forty-five minutes. Okay?

SIMON's face says it all – 'Forty-five minutes! You've gotta be kidding me!'

SIMON. Please… as quick as you can.

CALL CENTRE (*on phone*). Thank you Mr Rif… kind. Goodbye.

SIMON (*corrects her, frustrated*). Rif-kind.

SIMON *clicks the phone off, gets back in the car. He closes the door.*

(*Consoling himself.*) C'mon. You'll be okay. They'll be here soon.

He grabs a blanket from the back seat. He talks to himself a bit more for comfort.

You'll be okay. C'mon, just relax.

A beat of silence. In the deathly quiet, the reality of what he's done hits him in waves. He shouldn't have been driving and now he's knocked someone – something – down.

He almost starts crying.

SLAM! Something launches into the side of the car.

Silence. SIMON holds his breath terrified.

Again SLAM SLAM!!

SIMON *frantically puts the lock buttons down.*

Jesus Christ. Where's the?!

Frantically SIMON looks round for weapons, something to defend himself with. All he can find is the water bottle and a large road atlas which he tries to roll up into a tube. A truly pathetic weapon.

Right!

He also picks up a torch, which he waves around the car, trying to see who or what is attacking him.

(*Terrified.*) Hello.

Nothing.

Who's there?

SIMON *shines the torch and WHAM, there, by the car, standing in attack position is Woolly. As soon as the torch catches him he darts away.*

SIMON *jumps, screams and pathetically slams the map into the window about a dozen times.*

A scrabbling, scraping sound. Clawed nails on the side of the car trying to get inside.

SILENCE.

SIMON *is frantic.*

Suddenly the back door is wrenched open. SIMON *freezes.* IT *creeps in and slams the door shut. Once again, only the most fleeting glimpse of what* IT *actually is.*

SIMON *can't breathe he's so scared.*

(*Whispers.*) I don't know what – (*Corrects himself.*) who… you are, but I am so sorry.

A shaky, wheezing breath from the back seat. Suddenly the wheezing stops.

SIMON *slowly puts his hand on the front door to get out.*

He cautiously opens the door.

THWAKK! Two long-nailed, claw-like hands burst upwards and grab SIMON*'s shoulders.*

SIMON*'s face – a rictus of pure terror.*

IT. Stay in the car.

Beat.

SIMON. Fuck that!!!!!

In a flash, SIMON *is out of the car.* SIMON *is now in front of the car between the two headlights.*

AIIIEEEEEEEEEAGHHHHHHHHEEEEEEEEEE!!!

An ear-splitting sound fills the air. It is almost unbearable – the cry of the damned combined with the shriek of a burning elephant, with a hint of asthmatic wheezing thrown in for good measure.

The sound alone would be enough to wake the dead and loosen the bowels of every audience member.

In a flash, the biggest, most terrifying, dog-wolf fuck-faced monster drops from the sky, lurching down, descending on a screaming SIMON.

As the scream reaches its peak, the headlights blind us before –

BLACKOUT.

GOODMAN *and his lectern once again come up – we are safe again. For the moment.*

GOODMAN *is now wearing slippers and no socks. This passes unnoticed by all but the most astute and observant of audience members.*

GOODMAN. A sighting of a monstrous apparition or a 'hellion' is a rare thing. Anybody can say 'I was sure there was a presence in that church' or 'The room just felt suddenly cold', but to admit to seeing a monster? To swear to that experience requires such commitment on the part of the percipient, that they are taking a genuine risk. After all, people have been sectioned for less. In fact, in all my years of collecting these stories, Simon's account remains my only example of a witnessed 'hellion' and I cherish it for that. But let us be clear. There are no monsters. There is nothing lurking under your beds. One thing we can say for certain is that we're not living in some phantasmagorical dreamworld. No, what Simon experienced…

BEEEEEP – suddenly the stage goes red, GOODMAN *freezes and a piercing alarm screeches at us. As soon as it started, it stops, and* GOODMAN *continues as though nothing has happened.*

…is called 'pareidolia'.

A slide with the word 'pareidolia' comes up.

It's a psychological phenomenon whereby the brain takes vague and random stimuli and perceives them as significant. In other words, the brain, makes something out of nothing. We are pattern-finding creatures. We're programmed this way. We will find meaning anywhere rather than accept the obvious truth of universal chaos and nothingness.

As GOODMAN *speaks, he brings up a series of pareidolia slides to accompany his discourse.*

What we see, or come to believe we see, reveals who we really are. God in the clouds, the polar ice caps crying as they melt, Satan rising out of the flames of a car accident, a face in a shirt cuff and a watch strap.

But why stop there? If we're looking for them, then let's really look! A face on the moon. The devil in a pepper. Mother Teresa in a cinnamon bun! Hitler on your house, or even a monster in a tree. The 'monster' here is Simon's lie. He was driving without a licence, he's behaved irresponsibly and it's comes back to bite him. All he needs to do is admit to myself he's lied, he's done something he shouldn't have done, big deal, tell someone – if you need to. Move on.

You know, we toy, we dabble, we play with these fears from the earliest of ages and then don't like it when they scare us!

From peek-a-boo as a baby to the terror of being forced to play the Tenth Number – we –

GOODMAN *has dried, what is his next line?*

– we – we –

GOODMAN *finds it and recovers quickly.*

– push and push, testing the limits and edges of our fears. How far can we go? What is acceptable to us? What really frightens us?

GOODMAN *is shaken by his error. He takes a drink of water. After a beat,* GOODMAN *opens his mouth to speak and all the water pours out of his mouth and down his chin.*

This is effortless, it simply drops out, GOODMAN *doesn't even notice, he makes no attempt to wipe it up.*

The other person I think about –

Beat.

The third testimony I find myself returning to was…

GOODMAN *turns on his mini-tape-recorder. A light comes up on* MIKE PRIDDLE – *late thirties, smartly dressed in business suit – tie loose.*

He is the epitome of the city high-flyer. He is a loud, brash, insensitive broker, who could buy and sell you, me and all our families, and he knows it.

PRIDDLE (*on tape*). Mike Priddle – P–R–I–D–D–L–E.

The lights fade on GOODMAN *and come up fully on* PRIDDLE. *Behind* PRIDDLE *we can see a nursery.*

Priddle. Scandinavian name apparently. Think Granny was raped by a Viking. HA!

PRIDDLE*'s laugh is a cross between a barking dog and gas escaping from a pressure cooker.*

So Maria and I had been together for – six years? I'd just started trading, I was a natural, I seemed to have a 'sixth sense' for what was going up and what was coming down. Know what they used to call me, Mr Goodman? Huh? 'The Prophet.' Maria and I bought our first place together four years ago. Sold it and did very nicely, thank you very much. By then my bonuses were generous to say the least, so wallop, bought the four-bed in Notting Hill. Always stretching ourselves. More space than two of us actually needed but it's good to think ahead. Property's still the most solid investment anyone can make.

GOODMAN. Sorry, can you just tell me about the incident please.

PRIDDLE. Sure – er – Maria and myself had been trying for a child for almost a year. We'd come to it a little late.

Maria was determined to get her partnership at the agency.
And – um –

Beep beep. PRIDDLE*'s iPhone signifies an email has
arrived. He instantly grabs it from his pocket and looks at it.*

Got to do this.

PRIDDLE *turns his attention to the iPhone, quickly reads
the email and responds. He sends his email, it takes longer
than it should. When he finishes he hits send and we hear the
'whoosh'. He then holds up his iPhone to illustrate his point.*

Balancing work and family is tricky. It's a challenge. It's one
of the challenges of a modern metropolitan life. But what are
we going to do? You know. Not have a house big enough for
a family in a good area near good schools? HA!

*He laughs again. The laugh is awkward and affected. Yet
again it's as though someone has let three bursts of gas out
of a pressure cooker that might explode.*

Look, planning ahead, stretching are both key prerequisites
for any kind of happiness. That's why we have the weekend
place in Norfolk as well. Maria had found it difficult to get
pregnant and, er, we had done a course of a new IVF
technique. Our first couple of attempts hadn't worked, didn't
think she was going to be able to 'bear fruit'. Then on our
final go, bullseye, she fell pregnant.

PRIDDLE *reflects.*

Funny thing, I spent a fortune doing up that nursery exactly
how Maria wanted it, but she only went into it once. She came
running straight out all flustered. Said she felt… what was the
word she used… ? 'Uneasy', that's it. Wouldn't go back in.

Beat.

The first two trimesters were pretty good – but unfortunately
– early on in the third trimester, Maria started… spotting.

Beep beep. Another email. Again PRIDDLE *briefly reads
and talks whilst typing. He is oblivious to the insensitivity of
his behaviour.*

Doctors seemed to think that the spotting was due to a combination of Maria's age and her workload and decided to keep her in for a couple of days. Maria was of the view that forty-eight hours at one of 'London's most exclusive clinics' wasn't such a terrible thing – thank you very much, it's only money.

PRIDDLE *laughs again, the pressure cooker releasing three more bursts. He sends the email and pockets his iPhone.*

So Maria gave me a list of things she needed from home and from Harvey Nicks and I just popped out to get them. Just wanted her to feel that I was doing everything I could for her. Took me about an hour to do the stuff in town and then drive home.

GOODMAN. Sorry – sorry to interrupt. What time was this?

PRIDDLE. It was quarter to four. I remember it was quarter to four – because – the clock in the Merc is satellite-controlled. It's very clever. It automatically adjusts to whatever time zone you're in so if you're driving round Europe…

PRIDDLE *realises that he has become distracted talking about cars. During* PRIDDLE*'s next lines, the lights subtly fade on* GOODMAN, *who vanishes into the darkness.*

I remember thinking as I pulled in to the driveway – 'Christ it's a quarter to four' – I've got to get those contracts biked over to the office before five.

I went in to the house – grabbed Maria's stuff and my paperwork and then for some reason I wanted to pop my head round the door of the nursery.

He walks along a corridor and enters the nursery. It's lovely. There is a baby-changing station complete with tiny nappies, talcum powder and creams.

A bookshelf with all the latest baby-fad books.

And there is a cot. It's classic white and simple. We can see the sheets are neatly tucked in on an already-made little bed.

*A mobile hangs over it with farm animals hanging off it.
The cot also contains a little, red-dressed Tilly doll.*

PRIDDLE *walks to the cot and pushes the button on the
mobile. It plays its tinkling melody as the farm animals turn
and the lights twinkle.*

PRIDDLE *looks around the room. He gently adjusts the
nappies and takes in the sense of peace the little room has
been designed to create.*

PRIDDLE *is alone, soothed and at ease. He leans on the
changing table, takes a moment and smiles.*

The mobile's tune starts to wind down a little.

As the tune plays to its finish, PRIDDLE *moves to the cot
and leans in to pick up the Tilly doll. THWAK!*

*The pile of nappies on the baby changer is violently thrown
across the room by some unseen force.* PRIDDLE *jumps, did
that really just happen? He stares incredulously at the
nappies and then moves to the French windows to check for
a draft… as if that would explain it! Cautiously approaching
the changing table, he taps it with his hand – nothing.*

What force could have thrown the nappies?

*The audience start smelling the pungent aroma of industrial
bleach, the kind one would smell on a hospital ward. It fills
the auditorium.*

*He moves into the room, picking the nappies up from the
floor.* PRIDDLE *takes a step to the changing table, and as he
does, with a bizarre speed, the bottles, talc, wipes and
creams form into an impossible tottering tower – one on top
of the other.*

*He stares at this, taking it in. In fear, he tosses the nappies
onto the table, not wanting to touch it. He suddenly knocks
the tower of baby items over, they tumble freely onto the
tabletop.*

GOODMAN *appears again dimly at the back of the stage.*

GOODMAN. Were you looking at the nappies when they came flying off the table?

PRIDDLE. No. I had my back to them. I knew something was happening but I chose not to turn, Mr Goodman. My understanding is that a poltergeist is an evil spirit or an angry spirit. Is that true?

GOODMAN *laughs off this thought.*

GOODMAN. There's absolutely no evidence to support that.

PRIDDLE. Actually there was one other thing, a very strong smell of bleach. Not the alpine-fresh stuff that Ula uses when she cleans for us. This was kind of industrial, almost like the smell of hospitals. I looked to see if something had been knocked over when the nappies went flying, but nothing.

GOODMAN. Could you have been smelling something from somewhere else in the house?

PRIDDLE. I don't know what it would have been, Maria would never have had anything in the house that would smell like that. Besides, it was only present in the nursery.

Beat.

Anyway, the guys at the hospital said Maria was making good progress. They took us in for a scan but didn't want to show us, they said that there were –

Beep beep from his iPhone. PRIDDLE *is flustered this time. Nevertheless he answers it.*

Sorry – I'm right in the middle of this Japanese thing.

He sends his email.

Um – yeah. The scan. They said there were some distortions on the screen or something.

Beat.

Um – But they changed their minds and decided they wanted to keep Maria in for a few more days as she had some issues with her cell count. To be honest, Maria was getting the best care that money could buy and her being away meant I could have a little peace and quiet to try and close this deal. I was working through the nights – doing my best to cram it all in which didn't bother me as I've always been a bit of an insomniac. Although I was beginning to feel a little exhausted. But you try sleeping when your pregnant wife's laid up in the hospital, you've got a very demanding mortgage to service, two Mercs to make payments on, a twelve-pound-an-hour cleaning lady who doesn't do her job properly, on top of volatile and unpredictable markets. Not easy.

PRIDDLE *gives another of his pressure-cooker laughs. Three shorts bursts of escaping air.*

I must have fallen asleep in front of the computer.

He rubs his eyes and yawns.

CREAK.

A sound from the darkened nursery.

A beat.

CREAK. CREAK.

The sound of rustling cloth.

PRIDDLE *glances at his watch.*

(*Calling out.*) Maria?

The sound of the mobile's string being pulled. Its musical tinkle begins. This time it offers no comfort.

Maria? Sweetheart?

PRIDDLE *gets up from his chair and starts the slow walk towards the nursery.*

And now there is another sound, a sound he can't put his finger on… a loose flapping – like a forgotten shirt on a clothes line.

As he gets closer, the tune of the mobile warps, as the sound of the flapping becomes more and more frantic.

Fuelled by bravado, PRIDDLE *opens the nursery door, every bit the alpha male.*

As soon as PRIDDLE *enters the nursery, immediately all sounds cease. But the mobile is still swinging above the cot.*

PRIDDLE *approaches it – and as he does he becomes aware of what the source of the flapping must have been. The little bedsheets are in disarray – as if someone has spent the most troubled of nights there.*

PRIDDLE *is confused, what could have entered the room and turned the mobile on? He slowly aproaches the French windows. The curtains are drawn on them,* PRIDDLE *reaches out, slowly, cautiously and –*

WHIIP – he pulls back the curtain, revealing…

…nothing but the pitch-black night sky. He smiles to himself, and leave the curtains open.

PRIDDLE *feels ill-at-ease and can't get out of the room fast enough.*

He moves to the door as quickly as he can. The sound of an ethereal breath stops PRIDDLE *dead in his tracks. The flapping noise has begun again.*

The flapping sound builds and becomes more persistent. PRIDDLE *slowly turns – to see the unimaginable: the sheet in the cot is moving, stirring into life, almost dancing – the sight is mysterious, chilling, beautiful.*

PRIDDLE *looks on, hypnotised by what he's seeing.*

In absolute disbelief and sweat-drenched terror – he forces himself to approach the cot. This cannot be true – cannot be real. The swirling, flapping sound builds and builds.

PRIDDLE *reaches out his trembling hand and eventually touches the sheet. It collapses immediately, nothing beneath it. All sound stops.*

A brief beat – in that moment PRIDDLE *knows in his very soul that something terrible has happened to his wife.*

The French windows gently swing open. There, in the pitch darkness through them, is a figure. MARIA. She is dressed in a long white nightgown, her hair is long and her face a ghastly ashen white. She seems to be floating slightly off the ground – surrounded by darkness.

The lights in the room start to flicker.

PRIDDLE *doesn't know what to do – he cannot make sense of the madness he is witnessing?*

Maria? Why aren't you in the hospital?

This is no apparition. MARIA speaks. Her voice is strange and hazy, her lips don't seem to move.

MARIA. We are dead.

Suddenly she floats towards PRIDDLE. As she gets closer, she starts to float higher and higher. PRIDDLE cowers in disbelief.

As MARIA looks down on PRIDDLE she opens her mouth, and a wretched scream from the depths of her soul bursts from her, engulfing both PRIDDLE and the audience.

RAAAAAAAAARRRRRRR –

At the very peak of this scream, MARIA's blood drenches down MARIA's ashen face, painting her deep red.

A truly hellish vision.

BLACKOUT.

PRIDDLE *is back in his interview position.*

PRIDDLE. I managed to get out of the room. I don't know how long I'd been standing there when my phone rang. It was the hospital. I knew what they were going to tell me.

(*Laughs to himself.*) The Prophet…

(*To* GOODMAN.) …I got there as quick as I could.

His iPhone beeps. He takes his iPhone from his pocket, looks at it, but does not respond and then puts it back in his pocket.

I knew in my heart…

The iPhone beeps again, but for once PRIDDLE *ignores it.*

There is a shift in PRIDDLE.

Apparently the birth was… it ripped her in half. I'm glad Maria never actually got to see Barty. No one ever thought he would survive this long, but somehow life finds a way. That's what I've learned. Life carries on.

The iPhone beeps again – PRIDDLE *reaches into his pocket pulls out a gun and puts it to his head.*

The lights fade on PRIDDLE.

We hear a VERY LOUD GUNSHOT.

Lights come up on GOODMAN *at the lectern. The safety curtain is back in.*

A moment, then GOODMAN *clicks the tape-recorder off.*

GOODMAN. Whilst one sympathises with the tragedy of the Priddles' situation –

PRIDDLE. I'm not finished, Mr Goodman.

GOODMAN *is startled, the lights come back up on* PRIDDLE, *who is still in his interview position.* GOODMAN *is confused – as are the audience. This shouldn't happen – how can these worlds cross?*

GOODMAN. Hello? How are you…?

PRIDDLE. I want to show you something.

GOODMAN. I'm right in the middle of a –

PRIDDLE. Ah, ah, ah – I, want, to, show, you, something.

PRIDDLE *goes to the side of the stage and collects a tin can. He walks back towards* GOODMAN.

GOODMAN. What? That?

PRIDDLE. No, no, that's cat food.

PRIDDLE *places the tin of cat food onto the floor.*

I really want to show you something.

GOODMAN. It's really not –

The safety curtain rises, accompanied by a loud industrial sound. It reveals a large black wall with a single small door in it.

PRIDDLE *moves to the door and opens it, there is nothing but deep, horrific darkness through the door. He takes a step in, then comes back out and looks at* GOODMAN.

PRIDDLE. In you come. Don't worry, there'll be just the four of us – You, me, Barty and... You Know Who!

GOODMAN. Who?

PRIDDLE *goes through the door into the darkness. After a moment of cautious silence,* GOODMAN *walks to the door.*

Sorry – I was just in the middle of –

PRIDDLE *says nothing but reaches out, takes* GOODMAN*'s hand and drags him into the darkness. As they go through the door, it slams shut.*

The black wall now rises, revealing a new scene. The nursery has vanished, all there is on the empty stage is BARTY*'s cot.*

GOODMAN *is downstage in the darkness,* PRIDDLE *is upstage in the darkness – it is a reversal of* GOODMAN*'s position when he interviewed the other characters.*

(*Looking out in the auditorium.*) Hello? Can I go back now?

PRIDDLE. No.

GOODMAN. Okay. I understand –

PRIDDLE. Oh – you understand. What do you understand?

GOODMAN. This is a –

PRIDDLE. No, no, no. You said you understand. What do you understand?

GOODMAN. If you let me finish, this is a joke at my expense –

PRIDDLE. Oh this is a joke is it. I don't think you do understand. Do you – Jewy Goodman?

GOODMAN. I'm sorry!

PRIDDLE (*sung like a playground rhyme*). Jewy Jewy Goodman. Mummy fucked a dogshit.

GOODMAN *looks like he's going to cry.*

GOODMAN. You weren't at school with me.

PRIDDLE *just smiles.*

Who are you?

PRIDDLE. Who are you? Mr Brain-Box Clever-Clogs Overachiever. Living on his own, there's no one there at home. Dare you turn some of that prize-nominated, never-quite-winning acuity onto yourself. Professor Shit-Your-Pants.

GOODMAN *now looks like a scared little boy.*

PRIDDLE *gives a sudden sharp imitation of an asthmatic gasp.*

Desperate, GOODMAN *tries to laugh this off.*

Come on, Jewy. Six. Seventy-nine. Nineteen.

Another wheezing gasp from PRIDDLE.

Tell it.

GOODMAN. Tell what?

PRIDDLE (*fake bonhomie*). Come on. Unburden. How long's it been. Eleven. Ninety-two. Twenty. Time to tell your story.

GOODMAN. My story?

PRIDDLE. Tell it.

GOODMAN (*laughs, nervous*). Tell what?

PRIDDLE. Don't you dare laugh! You coward. You snob. You pleaser. So busy explaining away, forty-eight one thirty-two, everybody else's story. Tell it.

GOODMAN. Tell what?

PRIDDLE. Who loves you, baby?

GOODMAN. What?

PRIDDLE. Help me out, how old were you? Eleven, twelve, thirteen.

GOODMAN (*answering without thinking*). Thirteen.

GOODMAN *is shocked to hear himself say it.*

PRIDDLE. And who was there with you?

GOODMAN*'s mouth is answering for him.*

GOODMAN. There were loads of us.

PRIDDLE. Names.

GOODMAN. Freer.

PRIDDLE. Freer. Freer! What are the full names of these 'loads of people'.

GOODMAN. Nico Freer. Marcus Perry. And me.

PRIDDLE. Anyone else.

GOODMAN. No.

PRIDDLE. Really? No one else, that's hardly loads is it? Who loves you, baby?

Beat. With a terrible sinking moment of realisation, a name dawns on GOODMAN, *he now knows where this is leading.*

GOODMAN. Callahan.

PRIDDLE. That's his full and complete name is it?

GOODMAN. Desi Calla–... Desmond Callahan.

PRIDDLE. What? Dirty-clothes foster-home milk-money retarded hairless freak Desi Callahan? He's hardly forgettable, is he?

GOODMAN. No.

PRIDDLE bears down on GOODMAN.

PRIDDLE. What did you used to call him?

GOODMAN. I never called him that, that was Freer.

PRIDDLE. Not to his face no, but you said it plenty of times behind his back. What. Did. You. Call. Him?

GOODMAN (*ashamed*). Kojak. Kojak Callahan.

A moment as that settles.

It was after school, we were on the rec, chucking stones and stuff at the Echo. And Desi, Desmond, shows up. He was always hanging around in his dirty parka. He was desperate for someone to be friends with him. I tried to include him quite a few times actually but Freer wasn't having any of it, he was a bastard.

PRIDDLE. What next?

GOODMAN. Freer said 'You can be in our gang if you want', he just had to do what everyone else – what everyone else had had to do to get in.

PRIDDLE. Which was?

GOODMAN. The Tenth Number, he had to play the Tenth Number.

PRIDDLE. The Tenth Number?

GOODMAN. You had to go into the Echo, the stormdrain. There were random numbers chalked up along the walls, they were spaced really far apart. You had to walk in really deep to find all of them. The drain got much narrower the further in you went. Freer gave you a torch and told you to count off each number until you found the tenth number. Freer said you had to memorise the tenth number, come out and tell him what it was. Only then were you allowed to be in the gang. What Freer didn't tell you was… there were only nine numbers on the wall. There was no tenth number.

GOODMAN *hesitates*.

PRIDDLE. Don't stop now.

GOODMAN. So Desi went in. He was calling out each number as he went by it. He was so excited. You could hear him laughing and doing his clapping the further in he went. He stopped clapping when it got so dark he had to use the torch. We all knew when that was, it was the fifth number. It suddenly gets pitch black in there. It sounds different too, you stop hearing the outside world. I don't care how brave you are – this would shit you up. Even Desi – who never really understood anything, he didn't like it. You could tell. He calls that he wants to come out. Freer shouts back 'Don't you fucking dare. We're not letting you out of there until you've got that tenth number.' So Desi keeps going. Looking for something that isn't even there.

Pause.

And then we heard it. A gasping sound – a wheezing, gasping for air. It was getting worse and worse. It was desperate, frantic. Sounded like he was kicking his feet too. Maybe he was trying to run out, I don't know. It was horrible. Even Freer stopped laughing. And then it stopped. No more noise. Freer and Perry ran off, and I was left, just staring at the Echo, hoping that Desi was playing a trick on us, that he would come out.

Pause.

Next day at school they called a special assembly to tell us Desi had died. They said he was asthmatic. He'd been playing where he should not have been playing, and if anyone knew anything they should speak up.

Pause.

Nobody did. I walked home that night past the Echo. The police had strung lights up all the way in and covered everything in plastic. I remember the sound it made flapping against the brick.

The industrial lights in the auditorium flicker briefly and we hear the flapping sound of the plastic.

Pause.

It is just one of those things. A fluke. A horrible accident.

PRIDDLE. How convenient for you.

GOODMAN (*angered and defensive*). We didn't know he was asthmatic!

PRIDDLE. It wasn't a fluke that there were only nine numbers up there and you told him there were ten. It wasn't a fluke that you weren't human enough to let him play with you. And it wasn't a fluke that you didn't intervene when he wanted to come out of the Echo. No. The only fluke here was the fluke in his DNA that left him vulnerable to people like you.

GOODMAN. People like me! How dare you! I've spent my life trying to help people, trying to 'put back in', on an academic's salary – thank you very much. Trying to help people see the truth in amongst a sea of sentimental lies and crap.

PRIDDLE *starts laughing at him.* GOODMAN*'s excuses are pathetic.*

Don't laugh at me. I wasn't the one who made him go in there. I wasn't the one who called him 'Kojak' to his face. And I wasn't the one who wouldn't let him come out when he wanted to. I did nothing!

PRIDDLE. That's right. You did nothing. You passenger.

PRIDDLE *removes a pen torch from his pocket and shines it directly into* GOODMAN*'s eyes.*

Why not?

GOODMAN. Because I couldn't.

PRIDDLE *keeps the torch aimed at* GOODMAN*'s eye. He is relentless.*

PRIDDLE. Why not?

GOODMAN. Because I couldn't.

PRIDDLE's torch burns into GOODMAN's *eyes.*

PRIDDLE (*screams*). Why not?

GOODMAN (*breaks*). Because I was scared!

The secret's out. GOODMAN *stands there, spent.*

PRIDDLE *turns his pen torch off and returns it to his pocket.*

A sound from the cot – a tiny wet-lipped mewling.

PRIDDLE *walks to the front of the stage, bends down, picks up the can of cat food.* PRIDDLE *walks to the cot where the crying baby is, opens the can.*

PRIDDLE (*to baby* BARTY). Shhhh… shhh… shhh… shhhh.

BARTY's *crying gets worse, sounding more distressed, screeching like a wounded infant pterodactyl. The wretched cry is unbearable.*

GOODMAN. Is he okay?

PRIDDLE. It's alright, Barty. Daddy's got meow meow!

GOODMAN. Is he okay?

PRIDDLE *takes a spoon from his pocket. He puts it in the cat food, gets a healthy portion and starts to feed it to* BARTY.

Hideous eating sounds – like a rabid sewer rat devouring a pile of offal.

GOODMAN *can't even look.*

Is he okay? Please!

PRIDDLE *lifts* BARTY *onto his shoulder. Though we can't see* BARTY's *face, we can see from the swaddling that he is much bigger than a baby should be. The swaddling is filthy around the lower end, it is caked in shit.*

The one part of BARTY *we can make out is a large, pasty pale deformed arm. This is clinging on to* PRIDDLE's *shoulder. Despite the horror of the image, it is also somehow compassionate, simply a father and son. As soon as* BARTY *is cuddled, he gradually snuggles to sleep.*

PRIDDLE *comforts the blanket-wrapped* BARTY *and talks in soft, gentle tones.*

PRIDDLE. Oh Mr Goodman – for all your clever talk – your jargon, your limp analysis – you really are more scared than anyone, aren't you? What you've actually spent your life doing isn't 'putting back' or 'helping others'. It's been running from your greatest fear: That there's something more than the here-and-now and that every action you've ever taken – or didn't take – has had an effect. It's left a little trace, a ghost of itself. That's true, isn't it?

GOODMAN *nods. As painful as this truth is – it remains true.*

PRIDDLE *smiles at him and cradles the blanket.*

You know, Mr Goodman – our ability to confront our fears and deal with them, is so much greater than you can possibly imagine.

PRIDDLE *looks down at* BARTY, *kisses his little swaddled head and smiles.*

Shhhh. He's asleep.

GOODMAN. Shhhh…

PRIDDLE *slowly leaves the stage. Both he and* GOODMAN *shushing the sleeping* BARTY.

Once alone, GOODMAN *continues to 'shush'. He looks around the stage, there's nothing, just him, the darkness and* BARTY's *empty cot.* GOODMAN *slowly walks upstage into the darkness. As he reaches far upstage, he stops, frightened of what might be waiting for him in the shadows.*
GOODMAN *is now standing by the cot. He reaches out and touches it, at least here is one, solid, real thing he knows. A comforting remnant of normality.*

A thought occurs to GOODMAN – *instead of clarity being achieved, he is bewildered as to what has actually happened, where he is and even who* PRIDDLE *is.* GOODMAN*'s old self is reawakened, indignant at the humiliation he has just been subjected to.* GOODMAN *looks into the wings where* PRIDDLE *just exited and, with a burst of renewed energy, takes a step towards it, calling into* PRIDDLE*'s direction.*

Who the hell are you?

By the time the word 'hell' has left his lips…

BOOOOFFFF! The cot explodes into a shower of fragmented wood.

Emerging from nowhere is the most terrifying vision you could possibly imagine. White-skinned, pink-eyed, rat-toothed and totally bald apart from the odd wisp of pale white hair. This is KOJAK CALLAHAN *come to take revenge in his ragged, shit-stained, soaking-wet clothes. He looks exactly like someone who's been living in a pitch-black, cave-damp stormdrain would look. His dirty parka is zipped up, his hood hiding his face.*

A terrified GOODMAN *moves as far away as possible from* KOJAK, *who follows him, as he claps frantically and excitedly, almost jigging with demented delight as his asthmatic wheezes fill the stage.*

The black wall with the door flies in and blocks GOODMAN*'s escape. He and* KOJAK *are now downstage with nowhere to go.*

GOODMAN *is frozen to the spot – trapped in his nightmare.* KOJAK *advances towards* GOODMAN.

Callahan…? Callahan…? I'm so sorry.

KOJAK *dances.* GOODMAN *is paralysed by fear.* KOJAK *slowly advances towards* GOODMAN. KOJAK *jumps up and down, triumphantly clapping.*

In a blink, KOJAK *pulls the clothes off* GOODMAN, *who instantly changes into the green hospital gown the mannequin was wearing earlier.*

GOODMAN *looks down and sees his attire – there is a terrible moment of lucid realisation.*

Everything is silent.

Oh no. Not again!

The soundscape now kicks in with a force not as yet experienced, a mix of gasping wheezes, industrial machinery and the helpless cries of GOODMAN.

Please – not again – I thought this was it.

KOJAK *comes close to* GOODMAN *and hands him something – it is the hospital hairnet.* GOODMAN *reluctantly puts it on.*

KOJAK *now advances on* GOODMAN *again, he removes the face-mask from his pocket and hands it to* GOODMAN. KOJAK *insists and* GOODMAN *places the hospital face-mask onto his face, he does so.*

(*Frantic.*) I can't breathe. I can't breathe.

GOODMAN *now resembles the mannequin seen earlier in the* TONY MATTHEWS *story. He stands there for a second, paralysed and whimpering.*

(*Pleading.*) Not again. Not again. Not again.

KOJAK *drags him through the door in the blinder. They struggle for a moment, but it's no good,* KOJAK *is too strong, he drags* GOODMAN *through the door into hell.*

The blinder and gauze fly out, revealing a hospital room.

KOJAK *ferociously drags* GOODMAN *to the hospital bed and forces him to lay down. The sound is building to a deafening pitch.*

KOJAK *jumps up onto the bed and releases a primal wail as he melts into the bed.*

The lights shift to the cold white fluorescence of a hospital ward. KOJAK*'s cry transforms into the wail of an ambulance.*

The silent cacophony of a hospital surrounds us. The room is simple, the bed holding GOODMAN, *a picture of a forest on the wall, on a chair is a little Tilly doll. We hear the quiet sounds of a radio playing. It is the same talk show we heard during the night-watchman scene.*

RADIO DJ....–irlfriend of mine lilies. And she said thanks a lot – you know they give me a headache. It had the opposite effect to what was intended. Have you ever tried to do something romantic that's got you into deep water with a loved one?

The door opens and a white-coated DR SIMON RIFKIND *enters. He is on the phone and is talking on his mobile.*

SIMON. Yes I know I wasn't there last Friday night, Mum, I'm sorry. But I promise I'll be there this Friday, okay.

We hear approaching footsteps from outside the room.

Please, Mum – I'm at work, I've got to go. Of course I will, love you – bye.

DR RIFKIND *quickly puts his phone away, takes the clipboard from the end of the bed and hurriedly reads from it.*

DR MIKE PRIDDLE *enters. He is important and bloody well knows it. He looks at* DR RIFKIND, *who is holding the clipboard.* DR PRIDDLE *shakes his head at the junior doctor's clearly pathetic attempt to cram information.* DR PRIDDLE *puts his hand out for the clipboard, which* DR RIFKIND *sheepishly hands over.*

Mr Priddle.

DR PRIDDLE *glances at the clipboard. In a flash he has assessed the information.*

PRIDDLE. So this is Professor Philip Goodman. Admitted 3.45 a.m., attempted suicide. Failed self-asphyxiation in his car. Silly bugger, bullet in the brain – (*Adopting a Mr Punch voice.*) 'That's the way to do it!'

He gives his revolting laugh.

Resuscitation was instituted. Emergency intravenous infusion commenced –

BEEP BEEP. DR PRIDDLE*'s beeper goes off.*

Gotta do this.

It sounds exactly the same as DR PRIDDLE*'s iPhone.* DR PRIDDLE *reads the message and gives his now-familiar 'pressure-cooker' laugh, and carries on.*

Neurosurgical opinion quickly sought. Further examination revealed fixed and dilated pupils.

He takes a step closer to DR RIFKIND *and, in a patronising, tutorial manner:*

In. Other. Words, Dr Rif-kind?

DR RIFKIND *responds, though slightly nervous, with the tentative confidence of a recent graduate.*

SIMON (*correcting pronunciation of name*). Rifkind. Severe brain damage as a result of the asphyxiation, sir. However, in terms of an actual prognosis very difficult to tell. But if I had to guess, sir, it's a coma, a probable lock-in, here for keeps…

PRIDDLE (*cool*). Just one of those things.

Beat.

Let's just hope his dreams are sweet.

They start moving out.

Right, he's due in theatre this evening for further tests where we shall reconvene. Next room.

After a moment, an orderly enters, with cleaning apparel. It is TONY MATTHEWS.

TONY. Hello again, sunbeam. Don't mind me.

He wheels in a cleaning trolley, sprays some bleach onto the floor. Takes out a mop and mops efficiently – as he does, the waft of bleach hits the audience again.

After a moment he starts singing 'Why' – the Anthony Newley song heard earlier.

See you again tomorrow.

TONY *leaves, taking his cleaning trolley with him. As he goes, he whistles 'Why'. We are left with the image of* GOODMAN *alone in his comatose state in bed.*

As the whistling continues, the safety curtain is slowly lowered. We are forced to watch this condemned man in his bed as the horrific reality of his circumstances settle heavy on us. At the very second the safety curtain touches the stage –

Despite the fact we've been staring at him in the hospital bed, PROFESSOR PHILIP GOODMAN *enters suddenly through the audience – he's confident, relaxed, pleased to be there. There's a breeziness and self-assurance to him as he takes to the lectern.*

As he places his hands on the lectern, he knocks a pen off, which clatters to the floor. He bends down and picks it up.

He straightens up.

GOODMAN (*under his breath*). Good start.

There is the tiniest look of horror on GOODMAN*'s face, as though he knows it's all starting again.*

LIGHTS SNAP TO BLACK as a sharp deafening asthmatic gasp fills the theatre.

THE END.

NB. As the audience leave an announcement plays through the speakers in the exits:

ANNOUNCEMENT. Ladies and gentlemen. Please, keep the secrets of *Ghost Stories*. Thank you and sleep well...

www.nickhernbooks.co.uk

facebook.com/nickhernbooks

twitter.com/nickhernbooks